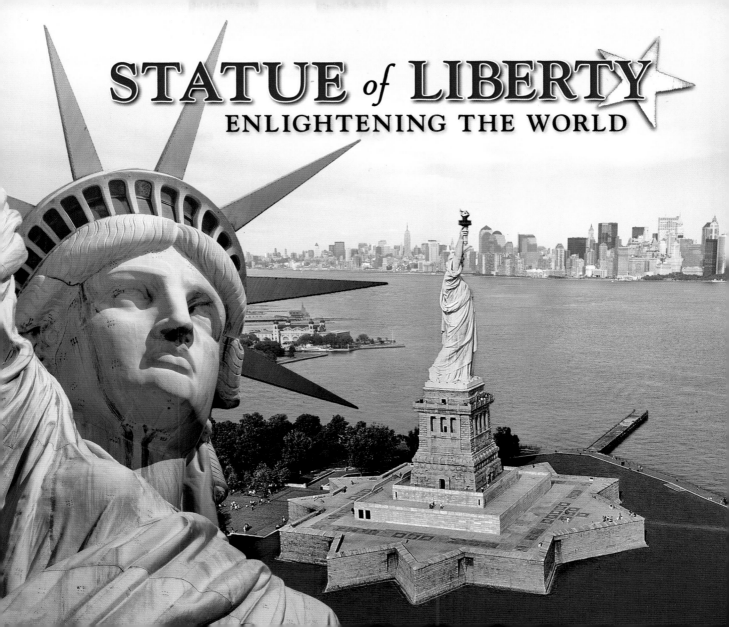

STATUE *of* LIBERTY
ENLIGHTENING THE WORLD

© 2010 Evelyn Hill, Inc.

Edited by Barry Moreno
Designed in USA • Printed in China • 08J0104

© 2010 Designed and Published by **Terrell**Creative
P.O. Box 34260
Kansas City, MO 64120

ISBN-13: 978-1-56944-393-4

Cover and title page: Select photo courtesy National Park Service
Back Cover: Photo by Joe Luman © Terrell Creative

Photo by Joe Luman © Terrell Creative

CONTENTS

Liberty Enlightening the World, mostly known as the Statue of Liberty, has become the universal symbol of freedom and democracy. She is America's most recognizable icon. In 1865, French Anti-Slavery Committee Chairman Edouard (René Lefevre) de Laboulaye, at a dinner party attended by French sculptor, Frédéric Auguste Bartholdi, proposed the idea of constructing a monument to independence and human liberty that was to be given to the United States of America to commemorate its centennial in 1876. At that time, France's own political situation was in turmoil. Laboulaye, along with others, hoped that a gift of such a monument to the Republic of the United States would send a strong message to their own country, while at the same time recognizing France's sisterhood with the United States. Bartholdi was commissioned to sculpt the monument; his plaster model of Liberty Enlightening the World was approved by the newly created Franco-American Union in 1875, and the process of raising funds began for its completion.

The statue became a joint effort of France and the United States. It was agreed that the American people would supply funding to build the base while the people of France would be responsible for building the statue as well as its assembly in the United States. Funding the project was a major obstacle to overcome. In France, money was raised through public fees and a lottery. In America, contributions lagged. It took editorials written by the famous newspaper publisher, Joseph Pulitzer, criticizing the rich for failing to finance the project, as well as the middle class for relying solely on the wealthy to fund the project, to finally bring in the necessary money to complete the pedestal project.

While monies were being raised, work on the statue proceeded. In 1876, the arm and the torch were completed and sent to Philadelphia for display at the Centennial Exposition. Visitors were charged fifty cents to climb up to the balcony. The money raised was used for the funding of the construction of the pedestal. Later that year the arm and torch were moved to Madison Square Park in New York City where they were on display from 1877 to 1882.

▲ The head and shoulders were completed by June of 1878 and were displayed at the World's Fair held in Paris. Great enthusiasm was generated for the statue, moving the French government to authorize a lottery to raise funds for its completion.

➤ The arm and torch, consisting of 21 copper pieces, were completed, assembled, dismantled and then packed into crates and shipped to Philadelphia where they were reassembled for display at the exposition.

Bartholdi chose the French foundry of Gaget, Gauthier and Company to construct the statue. They employed a technique known as *repoussé* to create the copper form of the statue. *Repoussé* is an ancient art of pressing or embossing shapes into metal, in this instance, copper, by hammering the copper inside molds. The sequence of construction was as follows: starting with a wood frame, then lath and plaster to dimensions of finished surface, and then a negative wooden mold built into which the copper surfaces were pressed, formed and hammered. Copper pieces were then riveted to each other, attached to the wrought iron supports, and hung on the structural iron frame.

Photo courtesy National Park Service

▲ Bartholdi chose the foundry company of Gaget, Gauthier and Company to construct the sculpture.

◄ Bartholdi decided the only technique of sculpture that would allow the statue to be shipped overseas was that of *repoussé*, which was hammering sheet metal inside molds, allowing for less weight. The foundry's craftsmen specialized in the *repoussé* technique.

FRÉDÉRIC AUGUSTE BARTHOLDI

French sculptor, Frédéric Auguste Bartholdi was born in Colmar, Alsace, France in 1834. The most famous of his works is Liberty Enlightening the World. From the beginning, at age 18, Bartholdi had a grand-scale vision, creating a 12-foot-tall statue of General Jean Rapp. His exposure to the Pyramids in Egypt also influenced his affinity for grand-scale art. Bartholdi's goal for the Statue of Liberty was to "… try to glorify the Republic and Liberty over there, in the hope that someday I will find it again here."

▲ Bartholdi also studied architecture and painting.

◄ Bartholdi at work in his studio. A small scale of the Statue of Liberty is seen on the left. It is thought that his mother was his inspiration for the statue's facial features.

CONSTRUCTION

▾ In this photo you can see Bartholdi working on the hand holding the tablet. Plaster will be applied over the wood frame. Then another wood frame will be built around the plaster. Finally copper sheeting will be hammered to fill the inside of this wood frame to create the exterior of the statue.

➤ Once the pieces were completed, they were ready to be riveted onto the internal frame structure that had been designed by Alexandre Gustave Eiffel. This process took place in the yard outside the foundry. This became a popular attraction for the Parisians; it is estimated that over 300,000 people visited the foundry during the construction of Miss Liberty.

Photo courtesy National Park Service

Photo courtesy National Park Service

DESIGN.

A. BARTHOLDI.
Statue.

No. 11,023.   Patented Feb. 18, 1879.

LIBERTY ENLIGHTENING THE WORLD.

UNITED STATES PATENT OFFICE.

AUGUSTE BARTHOLDI, OF PARIS, FRANCE.

DESIGN FOR A STATUE.

Specification forming part of Design No. **11,023,** dated February 18, 1879; application filed January 2, 1879.
[Term of patent 14 years.]

To all whom it may concern:

Be it known that I, AUGUSTE BARTHOLDI, of Paris, in the Republic of France, have originated and produced a Design of a Monumental Statue, representing "Liberty enlightening the world," being intended as a commemorative monument of the independence of the United States; and I hereby declare the following to be a full, clear, and exact description of the same, reference being had to the accompanying illustration, which I submit as part of this specification.

The statue is that of a female figure standing erect upon a pedestal or block, the body being thrown slightly over to the left, so as to gravitate upon the left leg, the whole figure being thus in equilibrium, and symmetrically arranged with respect to a perpendicular line or axis passing through the head and left foot. The right leg, with its lower limb thrown back, is bent, resting upon the bent toe, thus giving grace to the general attitude of the figure. The body is clothed in the classical drapery, being a stola, or mantle gathered in upon the left shoulder and thrown over the skirt or tunic or under-garment, which drops in voluminous folds upon the feet. The right arm is thrown up and stretched out, with a flamboyant torch grasped in the hand. The flame of the torch is thus held high up above the figure. The arm is nude; the drapery of the sleeve is dropping down upon the shoulder in voluminous folds. In the left arm, which is falling against the body, is held a tablet, upon which is inscribed "4th July, 1776." This tablet is made to rest against the side of the body, above the hip, and so as to occupy an inclined position with relation thereto, exhibiting the inscription. The left hand clasps the tablet so as to bring the four fingers onto the face thereof. The head, with its classical, yet severe and calm, features, is surmounted by a crown or diadem, from which radiate divergingly seven rays, tapering from the crown, and representing a halo. The feet are bare and sandal-strapped.

This design may be carried out in any manner known to the glyptic art in the form of a statue or statuette, or in alto-relievo or bass-relief, in metal, stone, terra-cotta, plaster-of-paris, or other plastic composition. It may also be carried out pictorially in print from engravings on metal, wood, or stone, or by photographing or otherwise.

What I claim as my invention is—

The herein-described design of a statue representing Liberty enlightening the world, the same consisting, essentially, of the draped female figure, with one arm upraised, bearing a torch, while the other holds an inscribed tablet, and having upon the head a diadem, substantially as set forth.

In testimony whereof I have signed this specification in the presence of two subscribing witnesses.

A. BARTHOLDI.

Witnesses:
C. TERINIER,
COTTIN.

▲ In 1879, Bartholdi applied for and received a design patent for the "design of a monumental statue representing *Liberty Enlightening the World...*" Patent # US11023 stands today as one of the most famous design patents ever granted by the United States Patent Office.

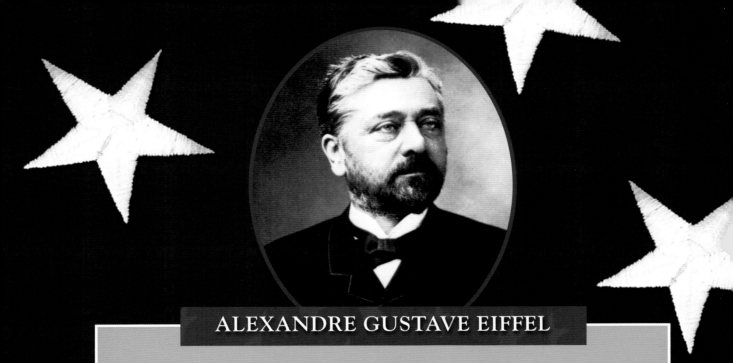

ALEXANDRE GUSTAVE EIFFEL

Alexandre Gustave Eiffel was a French structural engineer who specialized in wrought iron structures. His reputation grew when he was awarded the contract in 1877 to erect a wrought-iron bridge, 525 feet above the Douro River in Porto, Portugal. In 1879, he was chosen to design the inner support structure for the Statue of Liberty. He is best known for the tower that bears his name in Paris, France, a structure that when completed in 1889, stood as the tallest in the world until the Chrysler building in New York City was completed in 1930.

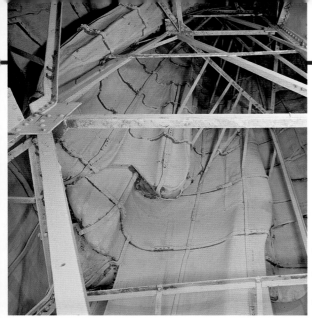

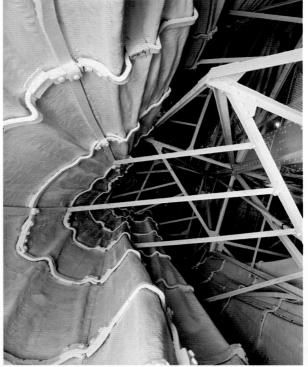

P reliminary work on the internal structure had been performed by architect/engineer Eugène Emmanuel Violett-le-Duc, who died in 1879. He was replaced by Eiffel who had designed the Paris World's Fair Exhibition Hall in which Liberty's head had been displayed. Eiffel's extensive iron pylon structural skeleton made Bartholdi's design a reality. This frame allowed the statue's copper skin to move independently but still stand upright. Eiffel calculated how much pressure each joint would need to bear and how to distribute the weight of the colossal structure. He instructed on site how to assemble each piece of the monumental statue to maximize its safety and longevity.

▲ These are interior views of the east side of the statue looking up that show the secondary iron frame that is attached to one of four central pylons. This secondary framework then holds in place the strap-on iron armature that supports the copper skin of the toga.

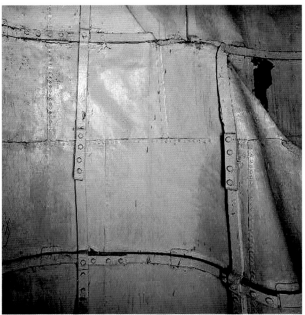

▲ The statue was engineered to withstand high winds. With winds at 50 miles per hour, the statue sways up to three inches and the torch moves as much as five inches.

➤ The pylon, or iron tower, is the backbone of the statue's skeleton. It rises 96 feet, 11 inches and it consists of four iron posts. The secondary trusswork is the structure upon which the statue's copper skin is attached.

▲ There are 354 steps inside the statue. Visitors can see the interior skeleton on the Observatory Tour.

RICHARD MORRIS HUNT

Richard Morris Hunt, 1827–1895, was possibly the foremost architect in America in the 19th century. He founded the first American Architectural School, co-founded the American Institute of Architects and served as that organization's third president. His greatest contribution to his profession was that he insisted that architects be treated and paid as professionals, on a level with doctors and lawyers. His many famous works include The Cornelius Vanderbilt II mansion; The Breakers in Newport, Rhode Island; the façade of the Metropolitan Museum of Art in New York, New York; and Biltmore Estate in Asheville, North Carolina.

In an act of Congress in 1877, Bedloe's Island in New York Harbor was authorized as the site for the Statue of Liberty. General William Tecumseh Sherman chose the site, which was Bartholdi's choice as well. On the island was an 11-point, star-shaped fortification named Fort Wood, upon which the pedestal would be built. Construction of the statue was completed in France in July, 1884. The cornerstone of the pedestal was laid on August 5, 1884. Work progressed well until the fall of 1884 when a shortage of funds halted construction with only 15 feet of the pedestal completed. Construction was resumed on May 11, 1885, as more funds were raised for the cause. The pedestal base, or foundation, measures 91 square feet at the base, 67 square feet at the top, and has a height of 52 feet, 10 inches. At the time of its construction it was believed to be the largest solid mass of concrete, above ground, in the world. The base rose 22 feet above the walls of Fort Wood, and extended below ground level another 15 feet to anchor the base. When pedestal construction reached the 29 foot level, four girders were built into the walls so that they formed a square across the inside. Similar girders were also placed at the 84 foot level. The two sets of girders were connected by iron tie beams which continued on up into the statue to become part of the Eiffel framework. It has been said that if there ever was a wind strong enough to topple the statue, it would have to overturn the island to which it was attached, as well.

▲ The pedestal is a monumental piece of work in its own right. The last stone was placed on April, 22, 1886.

Photo courtesy National Park Service

Circa 1938-1950

The original design of the pedestal recommended by Bartholdi needed to be altered when it was decided that the pedestal would be built within the walls of the old fort. Granite from Leete's Island, Connecticut was selected as the material for the outer wall, covering the massive shaft of concrete. The last stone piece of the pedestal was placed on April 22, 1886. The workers were so elated that they threw silver coins from their pockets into the mortar. It was now time for the Statue of Liberty to be released from the crates she had resided in for the past 11 months, waiting for her permanent home to be completed.

Photo by Joe Luman © Terrell Creative

EMMA LAZARUS

Born in New York City, Emma Lazarus was a gifted young poet. Early in her life and writing, she did not embrace her Jewish religion or ancestry. However, as the 1880s brought on the Russian pogroms and New York received many thousands of Russian Jew refugees, she became one of the first to champion for a Zionist state. Were it not for this backdrop of persecution and violence toward her people in Russia, the words of her poem "The New Colossus" may never have been written. At the age of 16, the first collection of her poems was published. Over the next 21 years, Lazarus' poems were published in many American magazines.

In 1883, Emma Lazarus was asked to contribute a poem for an auction to raise money for the statue pedestal construction. The poem, "The New Colossus" was singled out and printed in the Catalog of the Pedestal Fund Art Loan Exhibition at the National Academy of Design, in the hope that it would kindle a renewed enthusiasm for those working on behalf of the pedestal. Ironically, Emma was traveling in Europe, mourning the death of her father, when the statue was inaugurated on October 28, 1886. She returned home in September 1887, and tragically died two months later, most likely of cancer. Emma Lazarus' relationship to the pedestal and statue project could have come from her time spent living with her family in Newport, Rhode Island. There, undoubtedly, she would have come in contact with many of the people associated with the American Committee charged with raising the funds for the pedestal construction. Richard Morris Hunt, for one, was a fixture in that community, being the architect for many of the mansions built during the gilded age of the late 1800s. In 1903, her poem was inscribed on a bronze plaque mounted at the base of the statue.

Not like the brazen giant of Greek fame,
with conquering limbs astride from land to land;
Here at our sea-washed, sunset gates shall
stand a might woman with a torch whose flame
is the imprisoned lighting, and her name
Mother of Exiles. From her beacon-hand
glows world-wide welcome; her mild eyes
command the air-bridged that twin cities frame.
"Keep ancient lands, your storied pomp!" cries she
with silent lips. "Give me your tired, your poor,
your huddled masses yearning to breathe free,
the wretched refuse of your teeming shore.
Send these, the homeless, temptest-tost to me,
I lift up my lamp beside the golden door!"

—Emma Lazarus, 1883

The process of disassembling the statue into over 300 pieces and carefully packing them into 214 numbered crates began in January of 1885. Once packed, the statue traveled by special train with 70 loaded cars from Paris to the port of Rouen, where it took over two weeks to load the crates onto the *Isére*, a French naval ship specially commissioned to carry this special cargo to America. The *Isére* departed from Rouen on May 21, 1885 and arrived at Sandy Hook at the entrance to New York Harbor on June 17. It was a rough and difficult crossing; Miss Liberty had arrived. After the title papers had been transferred to General Charles Pomeroy Stone, the ship's special cargo was offloaded onto smaller boats and ferried to Bedloe's Island. The statue remained stored in the crates for 11 months waiting for its pedestal to be completed.

Photo courtesy National Park Service

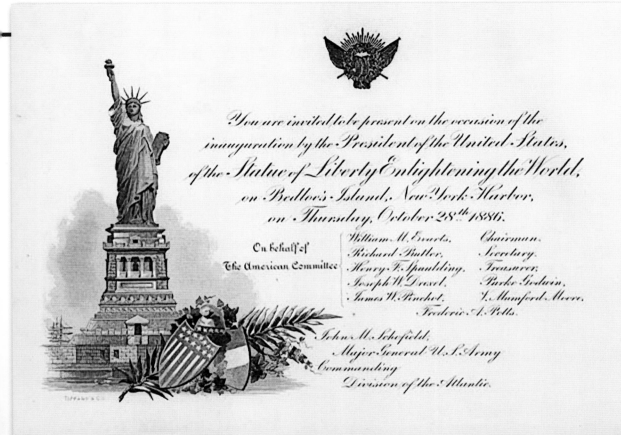

You are invited to be present on the occasion of the inauguration by the President of the United States, of the Statue of Liberty Enlightening the World, on Bedloe's Island, New York Harbor, on Thursday, October 28th 1886.

On behalf of
The American Committee

William M. Evarts,   Chairman.
Richard Butler,   Secretary.
Henry F. Spaulding,   Treasurer,
Joseph W. Drexel,   Parke Godwin,
James W. Pinchot,   V. Mumford Moore,
                Frederic A. Potts.

John M. Schofield,
Major-General U.S. Army
Commanding
Division of the Atlantic.

▲ The Invitation to the inauguration featured a lithograph of the statue and a gold seal.

◄ Iséere, the 215-foot-long French vessel, transported the 214 crates, weighing 220 tons, and 65 crew members.

Once the pedestal was completed it took only four short months to reassemble the statue under the supervision of General Stone, the chief engineer for the project. Bartholdi had traveled to New York the previous October to meet with General Stone to review the plan. General Stone, a West Point graduate and civil engineer, had supervised the construction of the pedestal, as well as the assembling of the iron skeletal system devised by Eiffel. By August, they were ready to begin attaching the copper panels to the intricate iron skeleton. Work proceeded quickly, and by early October, the work was nearly completed. Renowned landscape architect Frederick Law Olmstead, the man behind New York's Central Park, was enlisted to ready the grounds for the inauguration celebration.

On the night of the dedication, October 28, 1886, rain postponed the planned fireworks but it did not dampen the spirits of over one million people who turned out to celebrate the unveiling of *Liberty Enlightening the World*. Streets were lined with people draped in red, white and blue, cheering on the parade of dignitaries who each had a hand in the culmination of an idea formed 21 years earlier. Senator William M. Evarts spoke and upon the conclusion of his speech, Bartholdi pulled a cord that dropped a French tricolored veil from the face of the statue. A boy gave Bartholdi the cue after the Senator's speech, but was premature with his signal. Bartholdi, in the torch some 300 feet above, pulled the cord. Guns blasted, bands played, and the multitudes cheered. Senator Evarts sat down before he had finished his speech. Later President Grover Cleveland delivered a dedication wherein he stated, "We will not forget that Liberty has made here her home, nor shall her chosen altar be neglected."

Photo courtesy National Park Service

SHOW THIS TICKET!

INAUGURATION
OF THE
STATUE OF LIBERTY.

FOR STEAMBOAT
AND
ADMISSION TO THE ISLAND AND RAMPARTS.

Not Transferable.

▲ New York City declared the inauguration day a general holiday with over one million people in attendance.

1867

Bartholdi proposes a huge statue of robed woman holding a torch to be called "Egypt Bringing the Light to Asia" for the opening of the Suez Canal. The idea is not successful.

1875

Franco-American Union is created in France and approves Bartholdi's model of *Liberty Enlightening the World*. A formal request is made to President U.S. Grant to use Bedloe's Island as the site for the monument.

1871-1872

Laboulaye aids Bartholdi in a trip to America to promote the "Liberty" monument on Bedloe's Island in New York Harbor.

1877

President Grant signs bill designating Bedloe's Island as home for the statue.

1865

1870

1875

1865

Monument is first proposed in France by Laboulaye at a dinner party.

1876

Bartholdi begins construction of the statue. The torch and arm are completed, dismantled and shipped to Philadelphia for display at the Centennial Exposition. The hand and torch are then sent to New York City for display in Madison Square Garden.

1870

Bartholdi begins to design "Liberty" monument. Architect and engineer Eugène Emmanuel Violett-le-Duc begins concept of internal structure.

Photo courtesy National Park Service

1879

Eugène Emmanuel Violett-le-Duc dies and Alexandre Gustav Eiffel is named as statue engineer. Bartholdi applies for and receives U.S. patent for *Liberty Enlightening the World.*

1883

Work begins on the foundation of the pedestal, designed by Richard Morris Hunt. Emma Lazarus pens *The New Colossus* for the Pedestal Fundraising campaign.

1883

Édouard Laboulaye dies and is replaced by Ferdinand de Lesseps. Statue's arm and torch returns from New York.

1885

Statue is crated for shipment to the United States. It arrives at Bedloe's Island on June 17th. Bartholdi arrives in November.

1880   1885   1990

1880

Eiffel finishes design for the inner framework for the statue. French fundraising is completed.

1886

The pedestal is completed. Eiffel's skeleton is erected, and the process of attaching the copper sheet is begun. A decision is made to light the torch with electricity. Statue is unveiled by Bartholdi in ceremony on October 28th.

1878

The head and shoulders are finished and put on display at the Paris World's Fair in June.

1884

Statue is completed. It is formally presented to the United States in Paris on July 4th. First stone is laid for the pedestal.

1924

Statue of Liberty is declared a National Monument.

1903

Words from Emma Lazarus' poem, "The New Colossus" is added to the base of the statue.

1933

The National Park Service takes over administration of the statue from the War Department.

1937

Statue is closed for a two-year renovation.

1900 — 1910 — 1920 — 1930 — 1940 — 1950

1936

Statue of Liberty celebrates its 50th Anniversary.

1916

Black Tom Explosion damages statue and Ellis Island Great Hall. Visitor access to the torch ends.

Photo courtesy National Park Service

1941

Army MPs are stationed on Liberty Island to guard statue during World War II.

1982
Statue of Liberty-Ellis Island Foundation is established to raise money for restoration.

2009
Statue of Liberty's newly widened observation deck is reopened to the public.

1965
President Lyndon B. Johnson incorporates Ellis Island into the Statue of Liberty Monument.

2001
The statue and Liberty Island are closed following the 9/11 terrorists' attack. Liberty Island is reopened in December for visitors.

1960   1970   1980   1990   2000   2010

1984
United Nations designates Statue of Liberty a World Heritage Site. Statue is closed for two-year restoration.

2004
Improvements to security are deemed sufficient for full access to observation deck level of the statue.

1956
Through Act of Congress, Bedloes's Island is renamed Liberty Island.

1986
The restored Statue of Liberty opens to the public on July 4th, celebrating her centennial.

ILLUMINATION

Originally, the statue was intended to also serve as a lighthouse, and it functioned as such until 1902. During that time, the U.S. Lighthouse board was responsible for its operation. The use of the statue as a lighthouse was abandoned after attempts to increase the intensity of light by cutting holes and inserting colored glass panels in the solid copper torch failed. Originally, it was estimated that Liberty's light would reach 50 miles out to sea, but that distance was never able to be achieved.

In 1916, the lighting at the statue was significantly upgraded. Two hundred and forty-six projectors, each utilizing 250-watt incandescent lamps, were located in the star points of the old Fort Wood walls, as well as on rooftops of the buildings on the island. In addition, fifteen 500 candle-power gas-filled electric lamps were installed in the torch. In 1931, the lighting was upgraded with ninety-six 1,000-watt incandescent lamps enclosed in cast bronze floodlight projectors. These were placed in groups of 8 at 10 of the 11 points of the Fort Wood walls. At the 11th point, a cluster of 16 lights were installed in order to given heightened illumination on the face of the statue. In the torch thirteen 1,000 watt incandescent lamps and one 250-watt lamp were installed, approximately doubling the lighting at the statue. In 1945, the lighting was intensified again by the addition of 16 high-intensity 400-watt mercury-vapor lamps to the floodlight emplacements, which added a blue tint to the white flame of the torch.

▲ The original torch, replaced in 1986 by a solid torch covered in gold, now is on display in the lobby museum.

➤ The near right image (taken after the 1916 lighting improvements) and the far right image demonstrate how lighting styles have changed.

circa 1916

circa 1931 or 1945

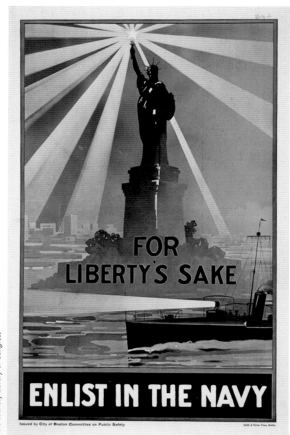

Photo courtesy Library of Congress

FOR
LIBERTY'S SAKE

ENLIST IN THE NAVY

Issued by City of Boston Committee on Public Safety

Photo courtesy Library of Congress

YOU
buy a
LIBERTY BOND
LEST I PERISH

A s the statue became a symbol of independence, freedom and patriotism, she was called into duty during times of war to assist in the call to service of the nation's citizens. The statue was used in the "Liberty Loan" campaign that promoted the sale of war bonds. The overwhelming success of this program during WWI led to it being used again during WWII.

LIBERTY CLEANING THE WORLD.

Photo courtesy National Park Service

▲ The statue's crown was removed in order to repair its rusted supports, 1938.

➤ President Franklin D. Roosevelt was on hand when the statue turned fifty on October 28, 1936 and presided over a rededication of the statue.

◄ Workers begin to remove the Statue of Liberty's nimbus rays.

Photo courtesy National Park Service

▲ Proposed master plan for the Statue of Liberty National Monument, 1939.

➤ Bedloe's Island, c.1950.

The statue underwent structural improvements in 1937 under the direction of the New Deal agencies, the Public Works Administration and the Works Progress Administration. A thorough inspection of the statue's framework and copper outer skin was conducted. The spikes on the crown were removed and rebuilt with new iron frames. Portions of the supporting ironwork had rusted and were replaced. Many of the rivets had loosened over time and were removed and replaced. The rusted cast-iron steps in the pedestal were replaced with a concrete staircase that ended at the foot of the statue. Also, the Works Progress Administration removed most of the army buildings and repaired the East Dock. A new public entrance was created with granite steps at the rear of the statue. In 1939, the National Park Service approved a long-term plan for improvements to the statue and to Bedloe's Island. The improvements outlined were substantially completed by 1965.

▲ This aerial photo, taken in 1933, shows the army post on Bedloe's Island.

▲ This aerial photo, taken in 1984, shows the improvements made over the years to Liberty Island and to the area contained inside the walls of Fort Wood.

Photo courtesy *Library of Congress*

In May of 1982, President Ronald Reagan launched a $62 million renovation of the Statue of Liberty for its centennial celebration, closing Liberty from 1984-86. It was discovered that the statue's head was offset about 24 inches and the shoulder around 18 inches from the central pylon due to a mistake made during assembly in Paris. Repairs included cleaning and patching of the exterior, replacing much of the internal structure and iron stairs, a new elevator and a new torch.

▲ Installed in October of 1985, the new torch was designed by Fabrice Gohard. The already luminous quality of the torch was enhanced at night by 16 flood lights.

► The torch is a symbol of enlightenment, lighting the way to freedom and showing us the path to liberty. Pictured here is the original torch.

◄ It required 5,000 sheets of 23.6-carat gold leaf to cover the torch. For three weeks, workers gently pounded the sheets into place.

Photo courtesy National Park Service

Photo courtesy Library of Congress

During the restoration of the 1980s, cracks in the right eye, chin and lips were repaired and missing hair curls were replaced. Also, a nostril was mended and detached shackles were repaired.

Photo courtesy Library of Congress

O n July 4, 2009, *Liberty Enlightening the World* reopened her crown to the public for the first time after September 11, 2001. In 2011, there are plans to retrofit the pedestal, which will take approximately two years. The crown will also undergo more restoration. This will enable more people per day to access the crown.

For over a century, Miss Liberty is still continuing to inspire awe. She gloriously stands apart from the skyline while being a defining jewel and landmark for New York City. What began as a gift of friendship from France has become so much more. She became the powerful and reassuring vision greeting immigrants entering New York Harbor, symbolizing hope and liberty. The Statue of Liberty is not just this iconic symbol to Americans, but to millions around the world.

Photo © Paul Thompson./DanitaDelimont.com

▲ The Statue of Liberty with Jersey City.

◄ The statue's tablet reads July 4, 1776.